# TORONTO

# TORONTO

CHARTWELL
BOOKS, INC.

This edition published in 2008 by

CHARTWELL BOOKS, INC.
A Division of
**BOOK SALES, INC.**
114 Northfield Avenue
Edison, New Jersey 08837

ISBN13: 978-0-7858-2458-9
ISBN10: 0-7858-2458-8

© 2008 Compendium Publishing,
43 Frith Street, London, Soho, W1D 4SA, United Kingdom

Cataloging-in-Publication data is available from the
Library of Congress

Printed and bound in China

Design: Mark Tennent/Compendium Design

PAGE 2: The immediately recognizable and beautiful Toronto skyline as the sun sets behind
the CN Tower and the downtown area *(Corbis C-118-0110 Lester Lefkowitz/Corbis)*.

RIGHT: Toronto's only castle, Casa Loma, was built in 1914 and attracts thousands of
visitors each year *(iStockphoto 1107021 Michael Preston)*.

# Contents

# Introduction

The view across the Toronto Harborfront today. In comparison with the earlier photograph from 1910 (see page 16–17) it is easy to see how the burgeoning water front town has blossomed into a thriving metropolis *(Corbis NT5466206 Alan Schein Photography/Corbis).*

# Introduction

Nestled on the northern shore of Lake Ontario is Toronto, the largest city in Canada. Not just the provincial capital of Ontario but also Canada's economic capital, Toronto—or "Hog Town" as it is sometimes known to its residents—is a densely and diversely populated city. Approximately forty-nine percent of Toronto's inhabitants are of non-Canadian descent and throughout its history the city has welcomed people from all over the world. This legacy has lent the city a colourful vibrancy that is as unique as it is successful.

Toronto's first inhabitants were the First Nations tribes of Seneca, Mohawk, Onieda, and Cayuga who all resided around this area, though there were no permanent settlements. Until 1788, European colonization was limited. The French founded a fur trading post, Fort Rouillé, in 1750 but deserted it just nine years later. Following the American War of Independence, however, the population in the area around modern Toronto began to increase. Many colonists with loyalist tendencies left the fledgling United States, preferring to remain under British rule. A large number settled around Lake Erie and Lake Ontario where those who had fought on the British side were paid in land for their services.

On July 29, 1793, John Graves Simcoe, Governor of Upper Canada, chose the site of Toronto for the region's new capital. Originally named York, building began on the eastern end of a bay formed by the Toronto Islands and the small town was protected by the nearby Fort York, built at a high point on the edge of the water. Trouble was not far away though. During the War of 1812, American fighters attacked Fort York, which was only lightly defended at the time. Realizing that their stronghold was doomed to be overrun, Canadian troops retreated after setting fire to their magazine. On exploding, it killed many of the attacking American soldiers including their leader, Zebulon Pike. Following that first assault, the defences of Fort York were strengthened and when the Americans attempted to ransack the fort again in 1814, they found it impossible and were forced to retreat.

In 1834, the town abandoned the name of York and restored the name of Toronto. The city was incorporated that same year and William Lyon Mackenzie became its first mayor. At that time—only forty years after the site was first selected—the city already had a population of approximately 10,000. Toronto and its mayor were also to be pivotal in the events of the Upper Canada Rebellion, when Mackenzie led an unsuccessful revolt against the British colonial government. Over the following decades that number grew rapidly as immigrants flocked to Toronto, with many of the new inhabitants arriving from Ireland. In fact, the Great Irish Famine (1845–49)

RIGHT: The stunning and powerful Niagara Falls are not are only a popular tourist destination but this mighty waterway has been a source of hydro-electric power for Toronto since the nineteenth century (iStockphoto 4590133 Brian Kelly).

brought such huge numbers of Irish Catholics into the city that by 1851 they counted as the largest single ethnic group in the city. Having escaped the famine, however, these people now faced discrimination and prejudice, which eventually led to large riots between Catholics and Protestants during the years 1858 to 1878, including the notorious Jubilee Riots of 1875. However, the strong Irish Catholic presence in the city became much more politically influential and potent as the years passed, thanks to the efforts of leading Catholic dignitaries, charities, and organizations as well as the arrival of more Catholics from Germany and France.

Growth continued throughout the late nineteenth century. As well as a population boom—thanks to high birth rates and more immigration—there was also expansion in manufacturing and agriculture around the area as the government opened up new parts of the western prairies for cattle farming and grain cultivation. Serving as the region's hub, Toronto developed rapidly. During the 1880s, streetcars and railways were built, while the Grand Trunk Railway and the Great Northern Railway joined together to build Union Station in the downtown area. It opened on July 1, 1893.

Progress was halted temporarily by disaster. On April 19, 1904 a large part of the downtown district was destroyed by a fire that began in a factory on Wellington Street West. It was first noticed by a policeman on patrol at 8.04 pm and soon became an inferno that took several teams of fire fighters nine hours to bring under control. When the fire was finally doused the city had lost over 100 buildings though, miraculously, not a single person. The area was quickly rebuilt and the following years brought ever more growth to

Toronto. Perhaps one of the most significant constructions of this time was the Prince Edward Viaduct. Completed in 1919 and designed by Edmund Burke, the system linked together parts of Toronto that were previously separated by a large ravine. The city's expansion was something of a mixed blessing for Toronto's administrators. With a blossoming population came a lack of housing, overwhelmed and inadequate transport systems, and—in

ABOVE: Toronto's core, the financial district, seen from the observation deck of the lofty CN Tower *(iStockphoto 5054168 Shaun Lowe)*.

some parts of the city—water shortages plagued residents. In 1954, to accommodate the ever-rising population and its needs, the government created the Municipality of Metropolitan Toronto. It was hoped that this system of thirteen self-governing councils would pull together to solve widespread problems. The system worked and, in 1967, the thirteen councils were merged into six; namely Toronto, East York, Etobicoke, North York, Scarborough, and York. Many citywide improvements ensued, including the installation of the world's first computer controlled traffic control system and the doubling of the area's water supply. Construction of public housing was also augmented.

By the 1970s, Toronto was experiencing a construction boom that saw many of the city's major skyscrapers springing up almost simultaneously. This led to problems with the old television and radio towers, which were no longer tall enough to send and receive signals without interference. The government tackled the problem by building CN Tower. Standing at 1,815 feet (533.33 meters) and completed in 1976, it is the tallest free-standing structure in the world and is probably the tallest structure that will ever be erected in Toronto. Other improvements to the city since then have included the revitalization of the harbor front during the 1980s when almost four square miles (ten square kilometers) of reclaimed land were transformed from an industrial strip into picturesque parks, walkways, exclusive apartment buildings, and hotels.

In a little over 200 years since soil was first broken, Toronto has become a world-class cultural center. Having left cultural clashes well behind, it is home to people from a smorgasbord of origins who help make their city a cosmopolitan metropolis of dizzying heights and welcoming, old-world charm and grace. With so much to recommend it, it seems likely that the future will hold yet more growth for "Hog Town".

RIGHT: The Old Town Hall of Toronto was completed in 1899. This photograph, taken in 1939, shows how even forty years after construction, the Old Town Hall retained its majesty *(Corbis U869439INP Bettmann/Corbis)*.

FAR RIGHT: No longer the most imposing building in the center of Toronto, yet still a firm favorite with residents, the Old Town Hall's detailed facades stand out in a sea of glass and metal towers *(Corbis CB023313 Shubroto Chattopadhyay/Corbis)*.

RIGHT: An aerial view of the Toronto skyline, shortly after the completion of the colossal CN Tower in 1976. The skyline has changed considerably in the following 30 years
*(Corbis SF37494 Bettmann/Corbis).*

FAR RIGHT: The skyline of Toronto some twenty years later. Taken in 1995, this aerial picture details the changes of the city's ever-changing face
*(Corbis 0000334579-007 Forestier Yves/Corbis Sygma).*

ABOVE: A panoramic view across Toronto harbor in 1910. The skyline is free of the lofty towers that fill the horizon of today's city *(LoC 6a22572u)*.

FAR LEFT: A view of Yonge Street looking north from King Street around the 1930s. The famous streetcars are visible in the distance and the city is obviously thriving *(Corbis BE043043 Underwood & Underwood/Corbis).*

LEFT: The view down a bustling, more modern day Yonge Street. This photograph, taken during the 1980s, shows a few of the original nineteenth century buildings remain but most have been replaced by more modern glass fronted stores and shopping malls *(Corbis NW007650 Nik Wheeler/Corbis).*

ABOVE: The Royal York Hotel was once the tallest building in Toronto and dominated the skyline when viewed from the harbor. Today the Royal York, at the bottom left of the photograph, is dwarfed by its neighbors *(Corbis LG006486 Lowell Georgia/Corbis)*.

RIGHT: Starting life under the name King's College in 1827, after a Royal Charter from King George IV, the University of Toronto is now one of the world's leading education centers with campus sites all across the city *(Fotolia 357706 SamSpiro)*.

Settlement (–1840)

Originally called King's College, the University of Toronto was established on March 15, 1827, thanks to the labors of John Strachan, Bishop of Toronto *(Fotolia 352731 SamSpiro).*

# Settlement (–1840)

Before the arrival of European settlers, the area around what would become Toronto was populated by the Huron tribes and before them the Iroquois, who had occupied this site for centuries. It is generally believed that the name "Toronto" comes from the Iroquois word "tkaronto" meaning "the place where trees stand in the water". The town itself was founded in 1793, when Governor John Graves Simcoe selected a site that was intended to supplant Newark as the capital of Upper Canada. The area was believed to be safer from American attacks as it was positioned further from the US border. Simcoe named the town "York" after Prince Frederick, Duke of York and Albany.

Despite its distance from the border, however, Fort York proved vulnerable to American aggression after all, and was assaulted and captured by American troops in 1813. The invading soldiers destroyed much of the stronghold and set fire to the parliament buildings during their short, yet destructive, five-day occupation. Nevertheless, when the war ended, Toronto commenced what was to become a long and steady growth. Incorporated as a city on March 6, 1834, at which time it reverted to its native name, Toronto boasted a population of 9,000, including many escaped African-American slaves from the United States seeking sanctuary in Upper Canada, which had prohibited slavery completely the same year.

RIGHT: An aerial view of Lake Ontario with Toronto in the distance. During early settlement, the shores of the lake were surrounded by swamps and what is now Toronto's harbor front area would eventually be built on reclaimed land *(Corbis LK006033 Layne Kennedy/Corbis).*

LEFT: A reconstructed example of a typical Iroquois settlement including the characteristic bark long houses associated with many First Nations, including the Oneida, Mohawk and Seneca tribes of this region *(Corbis 42-18429304 Marilyn Angel Wynn/Nativestock Pictures/Corbis).*

ABOVE: The military post of Fort York, first established in 1793, has been lovingly restored to its former glory. Visitors can see the old barracks, powder magazines, and officers' quarters just as they were in the eighteenth century *(Corbis DH011606 Dave G. Houser/Corbis).*

RIGHT: A close up on the main tower of the University of Toronto buildings *(Corbis 42-19301336 Richard T. Nowitz/Corbis).*

FAR RIGHT: Situated in downtown Toronto is the six-acre estate of Osgoode Hall. Now the headquarters for the Law Society of Upper Canada and the Superior Court of Justice, the building was acquired by the Law Society in 1828 *(Getty Images 56620210 Alan Sirulnikoff).*

LEFT: The Distillery District was founded in 1832 and at that time was home to the Gooderham and Worts distillery. The district became the largest of its kind in the world, exporting over two million gallons of whisky each year. More recently it has undergone a revival as a district for culture and the arts
*(Getty Images 71223079 First Light).*

RIGHT: Situated at 260 Adelaide Street East is Toronto's first Post Office. Built between 1833 to 1835, it served for only two years before the office relocated to larger premises in 1837 *(Fotolia 3864679 apeschi).*

# Growth 1840–1903

The Cathedral of St. James was finished in 1844 and on completion was one of the major structures in the city. The 305-foot spire makes St. James the second tallest cathedral in the whole of Canada *(Getty 200426361-001 Hisham Ibrahim)*.

# Growth 1840–1903

The late nineteenth century and early twentieth century heralded a period of rapid growth for Toronto, both in terms of population and construction. The city was a prominent destination for immigrants, especially the dispossessed Irish Catholics who suffered under the Great Famine of 1846 to 1849. By 1851, refugees from Ireland had become the largest ethnic group in Toronto. Unfortunately, conflict with the established Protestant population and the incoming Irish Catholics led to outbreaks of violence in the city, peaking with the Jubilee Riots of 1875.

Despite these troubles, the city began to flourish. A large sewage system was built and by 1841 gas lighting illuminated many of the main streets after dark. In 1849, the University of Toronto was created and in 1856 the first train service between Montreal and Toronto began. The Grand Trunk Railway and the Great Northern Railway joined forces to build the first Union Station in downtown Toronto. The coming of the railway dramatically increased the number of people moving into the city and also encouraged commerce. In 1891, the first electric street-cars began to replace horse drawn carriages. The nine-storey Temple Building was officially opened in September 1897 and was at that time the tallest building in Canada. Two years later, construction was completed on the beautiful Old City Hall.

RIGHT: Built between 1845 and 1848, St. Michael's Cathedral is one of the oldest churches in Toronto. The Roman Catholic edifice is situated on Church Street and was mainly funded by the donations from Irish immigrants
(*iStockphoto 4398632 Lorie Slater*).

RIGHT: The houses on Jarvis Street, often called the "Champs Elysseés of Toronto", date back to the 1850s. Their unique style made this a popular and lively residential area *(iStockphoto 681168 Mary Marin)*.

FAR RIGHT: St. Lawrence Hall was designed by William Thomas and completed in 1850. It was Toronto's first public meeting hall and was specifically designed to cater for concerts, exhibitions, and public assemblies *(Corbis BK002657)*.

LEFT: This early illustration shows the opening ceremony of the Ontaria, Simcoe, and Huron Railway in Toronto in 1852. The formalities were presided over by the Earl of Elgin *(Corbis BK002247).*

ABOVE: Trinity College opened in 1852 under a royal charter from Queen Victoria. It is now part of the University of Toronto *(Fotolia 1220991 SamSpiro).*

RIGHT: The Chinese population of Toronto now numbers approximately 400,000, but the first Chinese arrived in Toronto during the late-nineteenth century, following the various gold rushes in British Columbia. Once the railroads were built, the immigrants travelled east to find more stable work
*(Corbis 42-16711348 Rudy Sulgan/Corbis).*

LEFT: The Victorian Toronto Prison, also known as "The Don" after the nearby River Don, was constructed between 1862 and 1865 and on completion became the fourth of Toronto's jails *(Fotolia 4244233 SamSpiro)*.

ABOVE: Built in 1866, Spadina House became the family home to James Austin, president of the Toronto Dominion Bank, and his descendants. Today it serves as a museum where visitors can glimpse the lifestyle of a wealthy and prestigious family during Toronto's early history *(iStockphoto 2664641 Peter Spiro)*.

LEFT: The glass-fronted atrium of the Hospital for Sick Children. The hospital was originally established in 1875 by Elizabeth McMaster who was inspired by the example of St Ormond's Street Hospital in London. At that time it occupied a small, eleven-room house
*(Getty Images 56618870 Alan Marsh).*

LEFT: Completed in 1875, and the home of Knox College until 1914, 1 Spadina Avenue is a fine example of Gothic Revivalist architecture. Now it houses the Eye Bank of Canada *(iStockphoto 2400749 Peter Spiro).*

RIGHT: The supremely Gothic St. Andrew's Presbyterian Church was designed by architect William G. Storm and completed in 1876 *(Corbis 42-19301461 Richard T. Nowitz/Corbis).*

RIGHT: The oldest hotel in Toronto is the Gladstone. Built in 1889 and named after the street it stood on, it was designed by local architect G. M. Miller *(iStockphoto 1024525 Peter Spiro).*

RIGHT: The distinctive "flat iron" shape of the Gooderham Building has dominated Front Street since its completion in 1892. It was the first flat iron building to be constructed in a major city and heralded a design that would be widely copied elsewhere *(Fotolia 768737 SamSpiro).*

FAR LEFT: The Ontario Parliament buildings were completed in 1893 at massive expense to the Provincial Parliament. In 1903, a fire destroyed the west wing which was rebuilt in Italian marble *(Fotolia 1478553 SamSpiro)*.

LEFT: The imposing Confederation Life Building, situated on Richmond Street East, was originally designed by architects Knox and Elliot and completed in 1892 *(Getty Images 73259207 Donald Nausbaum)*.

LEFT: The Hudson's Bay Company flagship store on Yonge Street. This building was built in 1895 and originally housed Simpson's Department Store. Hudson's Bay bought the store in 1978 (*Corbis 42-15950775 J. P. Moczulski/Reuters/Corbis*).

ABOVE: Constructed in 1899, the elegant Old Town Hall now contrasts starkly against its background of modern skyscrapers. Today, it is home to the Law Courts and Justice Department (*Corbis 42-19301545 Richard T. Nowitz/Corbis*).

FAR LEFT: A detail of the neo-Romanesque façade of the Old Town Hall. Each tower and column has been sculpted with meticulous carvings *(Fotolia 372766 SamSpiro).*

LEFT: This is Yonge Street in 1900, already a filled with the everyday life and traffic of a bustling city *(LoC 3a00100u).*

RIGHT: This early photograph shows a typical scene of King Street looking east from the junction with Yonge Street in 1900 (*LoC 3a00099u*).

LEFT: Looking in the opposite direction, showing the view westerly from Yonge Street, is King Street in 1901 *(LoC 3a00097u).*

RIGHT: An early photograph of Queen Street in 1901. Nowadays Queen Street is a modern cosmopolitan area full of cafes and boutiques (*LoC 3a00095u*).

FAR RIGHT: A typical example of the Victorian-style houses of Cabbagetown. Allegedly, the area was so named for the many poor Irish immigrants who settled here and could only afford to eat cabbage (*Corbis DH011592 Dave G. Houser/Corbis*).

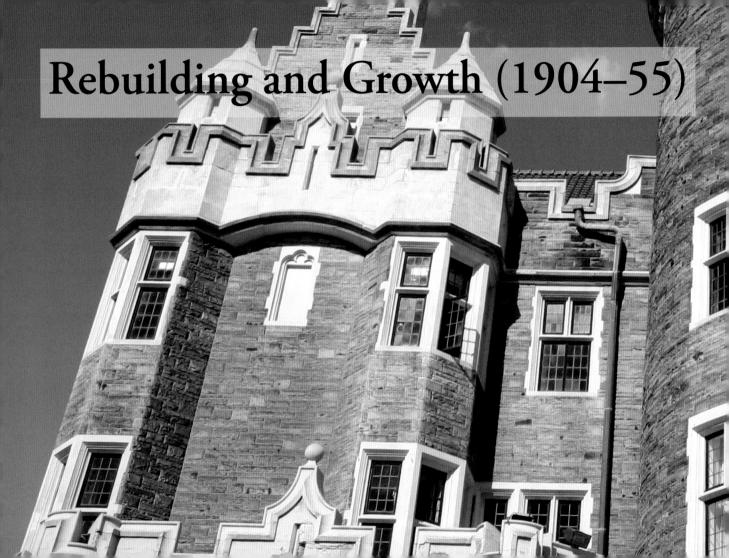

# Rebuilding and Growth (1904–55)

Toronto's Gothic masterpiece, Casa Loma, was the brainchild of local businessman Sir Henry Pellat. It was designed by the architect of Old City Hall, E. J. Lennox, and cost $3.5 million to complete (*iStockphoto 4717329 Jackson Lau*).

# Rebuilding and Growth (1904–55)

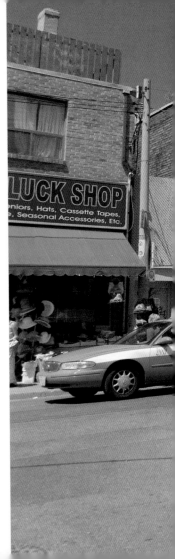

Following the Great Fire of 1904, which caused more than ten million dollars worth of property damage, reconstruction of downtown Toronto was quickly completed. The city had learned a valuable lesson and, as a direct result of the conflagration, the fire department was expanded while stricter fire safety laws were introduced. Such was Toronto's vigor at the time that the fire did little to slow its growth. Immigration continued at a healthy pace with Toronto now welcoming refugees from Germany, Italy, China, Russia, Poland and Jews from Eastern Europe. Many of these new settlers made their homes in the numerous shantytowns that sprang up around Bay Street, now the city's financial center. Construction work continued to improve amenities in the city and the building of the Prince Edward Viaduct amalgamated the city into a cohesive whole. Important buildings such as the Toronto General Hospital (completed in 1913), the Royal Ontario Museum (opened in 1914), the Royal York Hotel (opened 1929), and the Mutual Street Arena—containing Canada's largest auditorium and first artificial ice rink—all added to the city's reputation.

Following the Second World War, yet more people fled to Toronto from war-torn Europe, creating logistical problems for the already overwhelmed local government. To remedy the matter, the government formed the Municipality of Metropolitan Toronto, a series of self-governing districts designed to take pressure off the central governing body and encourage cooperation between the many areas of the city.

RIGHT: Founded by Eastern European Jewish immigrants in 1910, Kensington Market is one of Toronto's oldest and most multicultural neighborhoods. It was known as the "Jewish Market" during the 1920s and 1930s because of the high density of Jewish families living in the area *(Getty Images 56620693 Jean Heguy)*.

RIGHT: The view down King Street in 1910. Already, the electric cars that Toronto is so well known for, dominate the narrow streets *(LoC 3a00098u)*.

LEFT: A view of Yonge Street in 1911.
Horses and carts are still in use on this
busy central street, but the rails of the
newly installed streetcars are just visible
on the cobbled road
*(Corbis SF36044 Bettmann/Corbis).*

RIGHT: The Toronto Stock Exchange is the largest in Canada and the seventh largest in the world. The Art Deco construction was completed in 1913 and this older building was later incorporated into the design for the Toronto-Dominion Center *(Getty Images 3363408)*.

FAR RIGHT: Toronto General Hospital has been in operation since 1913 and this beautiful construction is the central headquarters. Situated on Elizabeth Street, the hospital has become a leader in organ transplants *(iStockphoto 1782528 Peter Spiro)*.

LEFT: Part of the University of Toronto campus, Convocation Hall was built in 1906 by the architects Darling and Pearson. It was modelled on the Great Amphitheatre of the Sorbonne in Paris *(iStockphoto 3438038 Arpad Benedek).*

FAR LEFT: Built in 1914, the CHUM-City building, with its terracotta Gothic design, is one of the most recognizable in Toronto. Before housing a radio station, it was the headquarters for the Methodist Church of Canada *(Getty Images 56620217 Bert Klassen).*

LEFT: Built in 1914, and formerly the estate of Toronto entrepreneur Sir Henry Pellat, Casa Loma took three years to build and was Pellat's homage to the castles of Gothic stories. It boasts massive fireplaces, hidden passageways, and tall battlements *(iStockphoto 1754246 Graça Victoria).*

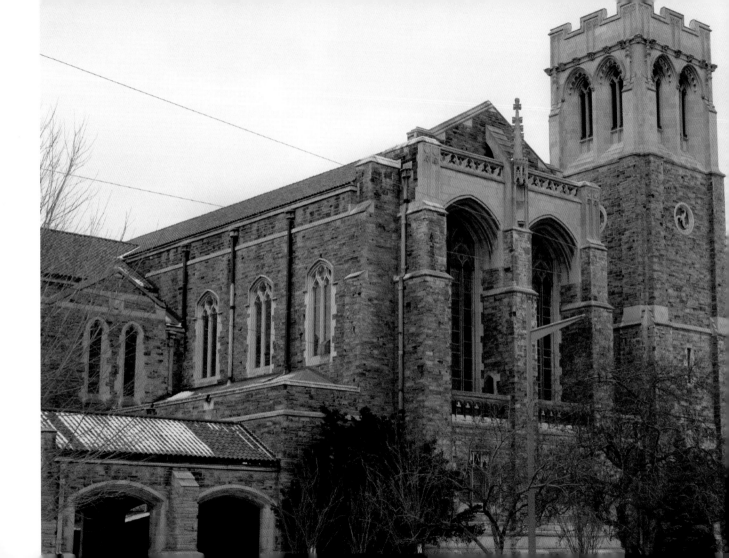

RIGHT: The Masonic Temple has always attracted music. Built in 1918, it has been a music hall, a nightclub, and was the venue for Led Zeppelin's first concert in the city. It is now home to MTV studios *(Corbis 42-16702156 Ully Bleil/Corbis).*

FAR RIGHT: The Gothic structure of Whitney Block holds the offices for the Premier of Ontario and many cabinet ministers. It was built in 1926 and designed by F. R. Heakes. When finished it was the tallest high rise in Toronto *(Fotolia 5224091 SamSpiro).*

RIGHT: The Prince's Gate was originally erected in 1927 to commemorate the Canadian National Exhibition *(Corbis 42-19301455 Richard T. Nowitz/Corbis)*.

FAR RIGHT: The exterior of the impressive Royal York Hotel, designed by architects Ross and MacDonald and completed in 1929. The beautiful Beaux Arts exterior was often the first of Toronto's spectacles that many immigrants saw as it was situated close to the main railway station *(Corbis AAGE001022 Rick Chard/Corbis)*.

OVERLEAF: The skyline of Toronto was once dominated by the Royal York Hotel and Bank of Commerce Building, which was for some time the tallest building in the British Commonwealth *(Corbis GNCA310 Bettmann/Corbis)*.

RIGHT: The plush interior of the Royal York Hotel has always been a popular stop for visiting dignitaries. The lavish main hall has a coffered ceiling supported by twenty-two ornate marble columns
(*Corbis AAGE001024 Rick Chard/Corbis*).

FAR RIGHT: Commerce Court North was built in 1930 to be the central office for the Canadian Bank of Commerce. It was designed by Pearson and Darling and was the tallest building in the British Commonwealth until 1962
(*Fotolia 3029434 SamSpiro*).

LEFT: Once the largest record store chain in Canada, Sam the Record Man was an institution in Toronto. Started in 1937 by Sam Sniderman, the chain sadly went into liquidation in 2001 when it found itself unable to compete with larger chains and internet vendors
*(Corbis RI002706 Bob Krist/Corbis).*

ABOVE: The historic Beaux Arts designed Canada Life Building on Queen Street was the fourth building to serve as a command centre for Canada's largest and oldest insurance company. Work began on the office block in 1929 and it was completed in 1931 *(iStockphoto 4829838 Arpad Benedek).*

RIGHT: Toronto City Centre Airport opened in 1939 on the Toronto Islands. During the Second World War, it became a training centre for pilots from the Royal Canadian and Royal Norwegian Air Forces and is now used for civil aviation *(Fotolia 4816792 Gary Blakeley).*

FAR LEFT: The Hockey Hall of Fame is a museum devoted to the nation's favourite sport. Established in 1945, the museum contains many historic exhibits including the Stanley Cup donated by Lord Stanley *(iStockphoto 4050577 Arpad Benedek).*

LEFT: The Princess Margaret Hospital was founded in 1952 and specializes in all forms of oncology. It has established itself as a world famous teaching hospital *(Fotolia 357781 SamSpiro).*

# Urban Renewal (1955–90)

The latter part of the twentieth century witnessed a huge growth in Toronto; in particular the financial district achieved new heights both in size and importance (iStockphoto 1360429 Emilia Kun).

# Urban Renewal (1955–90)

Throughout the decades following the mid-point of the twentieth century Toronto continued to blossom, becoming a city of international importance. Irish and British immigrants continued to make Toronto their new home, swelling the population to more than one million by the 1950s for the first time. The end of 1954 saw the completion of Toronto's first section of subway and in the following years work began on some of the city's major roads, such as Highway 401 in 1956 and the Gardiner Expressway in 1955. The city center also began a period of renewal. New City Hall opened in 1965 amid much controversy. Many residents disliked the ultra-modern look of the building designed by Finnish architect Viljo Revell and preferred the regal splendour of the original town hall.

Other notable buildings completed during this period in Toronto's history include the CN Tower, the McLaughlin Planetarium, and the Ontario Science Center. Sports arenas also moved with the times, making Toronto a hub for world class sporting events. The Sky Dome opened in 1989, the world's first open air arena with a fully retractable roof. The world's largest shopping mall, the Eaton Center, was also opened on Yonge Street. By 1971, the population had doubled again to more than two million, with Toronto becoming the number one destination for immigrants in Canada.

ABOVE: During the 1960s, Yorkville was the place for the "flower power" generation to hang out, drink coffee, and even meet the rock stars of the era who occasionally performed here (*Getty Images 56620723 Alan Marsh*).

RIGHT: Just one of the many pathways available to pedestrians. Begun in the 1960s by city planner Matthew Lawson, the system was designed to solve the overcrowding of the city's sidewalks and encourage small businesses which were otherwise being squeezed out of existence by the high rise towers (*iStockphoto 4984724 Adam Korzekwa*).

RIGHT: The new City Hall was completed in 1964 and initially disliked by many residents. Designed by celebrated architect Viljo Revell, the curved towers frame a circular building which acts as a rendezvous point for the many Toronto district councils (*Fotolia 414613 SamSpiro*).

FAR RIGHT: Named after a former major of Toronto, Nathan Phillips Square was opened in 1965 and has become popular with local residents when it is transformed into an ice rink each winter (*iStockphoto 4849736 Arpad Benedek*).

RIGHT: The Gardiner Expressway connects downtown Toronto with its western suburbs. Work on the route began in 1955 and was completed in 1966. It was one of the first major projects to be undertaken by the newly formed Metro Toronto government (*Getty Images sb10065135g-001 Finn O'Hara*).

FAR RIGHT: The Ontario Science Center was designed by local architect Raymond Moriyama and built alongside the Don River. It was due to be completed in 1967 to complement the celebrations of Toronto's bicentennial, but construction was unfortunately not finished until 1969 (*Corbis DH011604 Dave G. Houser/Corbis*).

OVERLEAF: Honest Ed's is a celebrated landmark in Toronto. Ed Mirvish slowly bought up the Victorian homes on the east side of the block between 1959 and 1963 and converted them into shops, cafes, bookshops, and art galleries (*Getty Images 56620233 Ron Watts*).

ABOVE: The geodesic dome of Ontario Place opened in 1971 and was part of a seasonal amusement park situated on the shore of Lake Ontario. The dome houses an IMAX cinema similar to that of the Epcot Centre in Disneyland *(Getty Images 72195493 Cylla Von Tiedemann).*

RIGHT: An aerial shot of Ontario Place, an amusement park that includes walking trails winding over artificially landscaped islands. Situated on the shore of Lake Ontario, it specializes in children's activities *(iStockphoto 4333929 Gary Blakeley).*

ABOVE: Just across from Old City Hall is Sheraton Center Hotel. Standing at a moderate 443 feet (135 meters) high and completed in 1972, it is located next to the similarly styled Thompson Building, which was also completed in 1972. Both are part of the Queen Bay Center *(iStockphoto 3999134 Arpad Benedek).*

RIGHT: Part of the University of Toronto, Robarts Library opened in 1973 and is now the largest book repository in Canada *(iStockphoto 1621710 Peter Spiro).*

LEFT: The CN Tower mid way through construction on November 13, 1973. When completed the tower was designed to act as a massive TV and radio tower, as well as boasting a restaurant and observation deck for the public *(Corbis U1789346 Bettmann/Corbis).*

LEFT: The last of the concrete is poured on top of the nearly completed CN Tower on February 22, 1974. Costing twenty-one million dollars to build, the CN Tower would soon be the world's largest free-standing structure *(Corbis U1798014 Bettmann/Corbis).*

RIGHT: A Sikorsky CH-54 helicopter carries pieces of a crane from the top of CN Tower on March 8, 1975 (*Corbis U1831240 Bettmann/Corbis*).

FAR RIGHT: The completed CN Tower dominates the skyline of Toronto. From its viewing gallery visitors can see 100 miles across the surrounding landscape on a clear day (*iStockphoto 734318 Sang Nguyen*).

FAR LEFT: The towering edifice of the First Bank Tower, or First Canadian Place, was completed in 1976 and has a staggering seventy-two floors. Standing next to it is the equally impressive golden Scotia Plaza Tower, which was erected twelve years later in 1986 *(Corbis 42-16711909 Rudy Sulgan/Corbis).*

LEFT: The unique Royal Bank Plaza Towers, built in 1976, stand out against the surrounding buildings thanks to their golden hue. The color is actually made with real gold. Each window is coated with a twenty-four carat layer *(Fotolia 2699629 Alexandar Iotzov).*

LEFT: Standing outside Union Station is a sculpture dedicated to multiculturalism, an issue on which Toronto has provided an example to the rest of the world *(Corbis 42-16711086 Rudy Sulgan/Corbis).*

ABOVE: The Sun Life Center West was built in 1983 when the successful insurance company moved its headquarters from Montreal to Toronto. It has twenty-four floors but even at 360 feet (110 meters) high, it is nowhere near the tallest tower in the city *(Corbis 0000231190-007 Jacques Langevin/Corbis Sygma).*

FAR LEFT: Front Street, once in the *Guinness Book of Records* for being the longest road in the world, is lined with many important buildings including the CN Tower, Union Street Station, and the Metro Convention Center (pictured). Completed in 1984 the center is used for many important national events, including the filming of *Canadian Idol* (iStockphoto 4833696 Arpad Benedek).

LEFT: At one time Queen Street was a rundown warehouse district but, since the 1980s, it has undergone a revival and been reinvented as a haven for cafés, bars, and quirky boutiques (Corbis RI002704 Bob Krist/Corbis).

RIGHT: One of the recently added pedestrian tunnels in Union Station. These glass-surrounded walkways enable passengers to walk to many of the downtown office towers without having to brave the elements *(Corbis AABL001088 Jon Hicks/Corbis).*

LEFT: The Rogers Center, the first stadium in the world to have a completely retractable roof, was officially opened in 1989 *(Getty Images 412568-004 John Edwards)*.

ABOVE: The Rogers Center illuminated at night is a stunning sight. It is alleged that the stadium uses enough power to light the entire province of Prince Edward Island *(Getty Images 73259299 Dennis McColeman)*.

Almost as tall as First Canadian Place, its neighbor—the unique Scotia Plaza—stands at 902 feet (275 meters) and was completed in 1989 *(iStockphoto 785483 Jon Tarrant).*

An aerial shot looking out over the harbor area and across a magnificent, frozen Lake Ontario. Many of the luxury apartment blocks that now line the shore had yet to be completed (Corbis SP012983 Robert Estall/Corbis).

# Recent Developments (1990–)

The panorama of Toronto is distinguished by CN Tower, a feat of Canadian engineering that dominates every view *(iStockphoto 3350936 Tony Tremblay)*.

# Recent Developments (1990–)

Toronto has become a huge metropolis sprawling across 100 square miles. One of Canada's most dynamic cities, with a population that has doubled once again since the early 1970s to over four million and home to over 100 different ethnic groups, it is the richest city in the country; a fact that is reflected in its confident architecture and excellent services. Today's Toronto also boasts a wealth of museums, art galleries, stadiums, a world-class university, and a city center that has attracted admiration from around the globe. Many of the towering skyscrapers of Toronto are on the cutting edge of modern architecture, with buildings such as those of Brookfield Place or the soon to be completed Trump International Hotel and Tower.

This period has also seen a massive revitalization of "Old Toronto" with many of the older and more rundown buildings receiving extensive redevelopments; the Royal Ontario Museum, the Gardiner Museum and the Ontario College of Art and Design are just a few examples. Several of the poorer districts have been renovated and reinvented in recent years, including the Distillery district and the Beaches.

RIGHT: The cavernous Eaton Center shopping mall is the largest in Canada. The first stage of construction opened to the public in 1977 and the final stages were eventually finished in 1990 *(iStockphoto 1200710 Dean Tomlinson)*.

ABOVE: Inside the ultra modern and giant Eaton Center. It is said that anything available for sale in the world can be bought here *(Corbis 42-19301452 Richard T. Nowitz/Corbis)*.

ABOVE: Once the most imposing building in Front East Street, the Gooderham Building is now dwarfed by the surrounding skyscrapers of Brookfield Place, a forty-seven storey tower completed in 1991 *(Getty Images 76208290 Glenn van der Knijff)*.

RIGHT: The neck-breaking view of the shimmering Royal Bank Plaza and its neighbor, Brookfield Place, from the ground. The total value of the gold contained in the windows of the Plaza is $1,000,000
*(iStockphoto 776785 Jon Tarrant).*

FAR RIGHT: The 250 Tower, part of the Eaton Center on Yonge Street, was completed in 1992 and its unique design was envisaged by Crang and Boake architects
*(iStockphoto 3239648 Roger Lecuyer).*

LEFT: The Humber Bay Arch Bridge or "the Gateway" is a pedestrian and cycle bridge spanning the Humber River. It was completed in the mid 1990s and connects "Old Toronto" to the Etobicoke district *(iStockphoto 4732547 Grzegorz Malec).*

LEFT: The breathtaking scenery from the top of CN Tower. The viewing platform also has an area of floor made from reinforced glass for those visitors brave enough to stand on it and look straight down *(Corbis FF002710 Franz-Marc Frei/Corbis)*.

ABOVE: Looking out across the many skyscrapers of downtown Toronto and the north shore of Lake Ontario, it is easy to see how the city has grown not only in size but also in height *(iStockphoto 4492339 Gary Blakeley)*.

FAR LEFT: An aerial view of the expansive suburbs of Toronto. The city now covers an area of 100 square miles *(iStockphoto 4587424 Niko Vujevic).*

LEFT: Yonge Street has retained a few of its older buildings, but most of the nineteenth century low-rise constructions have been replaced with glittering skyscrapers *(iStockphoto 2618625 roger lecuyer).*

RIGHT: The National Trade Center is an exhibition and conference venue that hosts over 180 shows every year and has won many awards for excellence in this field. The center opened in 1997 and covers a million square feet of useable space *(Fotolia 357785 SamSpiro).*

FAR RIGHT: The Postal Delivery Building was renovated in 1997 and is now a top sports stadium called the Air Canada Center *(Corbis 0000231190-001 Jacques Langevin/Corbis Sygma).*

RIGHT: Home to the Toronto Symphony Orchestra is the futuristic Roy Thompson Hall. Built in 1982, but completely restored in 2002, the hall has a capacity of 2,630 and an inbuilt pipe organ *(Getty Images 78016445 J. A. Kraulis).*

LEFT: The Ontario School of Art was initially founded in 1876 but this particular section, called the Sharp Center for Design, was added in 2004 and designed by Will Alsop *(Corbis 42-17901673 Arcaid/Corbis).*

RIGHT: A ferry pushes its way through the frozen waters of Queen's Quay in Toronto's waterfront district. This area has undergone a massive transformation in recent years with ever more high-rise luxury apartment blocks being built *(Fotolia 2461987 Orchidpoet).*

RIGHT: The lofty Scotia Plaza and the newly completed hotel "1 King West" dominate the skyline in this Toronto street. 1 King West was completed in 2005 and has 51 floors *(iStockphoto 3354674 Tony Tremblay).*

RIGHT: The Royal Ontario Museum undergoes a revamp as construction workers begin piecing together the eye-catching "Crystal" designed by architect Daniel Libeskind *(iStockphoto 3353385 Joe Lepiano).*

RIGHT: There has been a Royal Ontario Museum in the city since 1914 but this particular section, known as "the Crystal", is due to be completed in 2010 though sections are open to the public today *(Getty Images Sb10065355t-001 Donald Nausbaum).*

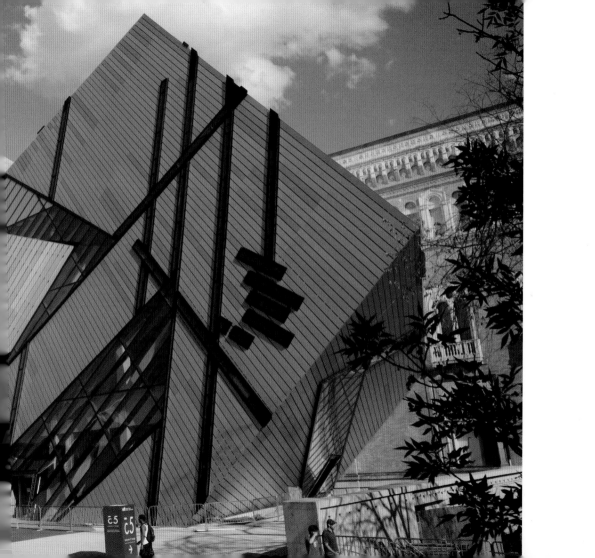

ABOVE: The bright lights and bustle of modern day Yonge Street, south of Gerrard Street. In comparison with the earlier photographs from the 1900s, it is easy to see how the city has changed (*Getty Images 78175855 Brian Summers*).

RIGHT: In Toronto, old buildings now stand side by side with the ultra modern (*Fotolia 328226 Dragan Trifunovic*).

FAR RIGHT: Queen Street has maintained an interesting mix of old buildings and new skyscrapers (*iStockphoto 737448 Olga Skalkina*).

LEFT: A suburb of East York in Toronto, Beaches is a quiet area that has managed to hold on to much of its old world charm. Today, it is known for its colorful shop fronts and its excellent restaurants *(Getty Images 56618804 Alan Marsh).*

LEFT: Thanks to an enviable example of harmonious cosmopolitan living, Toronto has seen the appearance of many non-Christian houses of worship. This Hindu Temple is just one impressive example *(Fotolia 3944636 Peter Guzas).*

ABOVE: Looking inland toward the suburbs of Toronto from a vantage point near St. James Cathedral *(Corbis 0000231190-016 Jacques Langevin/Corbis Sygma).*

LEFT: Toronto's financial district is a maze of soaring towers and quaint nineteenth century buildings
*(Getty Images 78175862 Brian Summers).*

ABOVE: Toronto's marina has become an increasingly sought after residential area with its many expensive apartment blocks completed every year *(iStockphoto 1667970 Peter Spiro)*.

RIGHT: Just one of the many plazas situated in downtown Toronto that are so conducive to the community spirit and relaxed attitude that has made the city one of the number one places in which to live *(iStockphoto 4833282 Arpad Benedek)*.

# Index